Letts
gets you through

KS2
SPELLING
SATs SUCCESS
WORKBOOK

Ages 9–11

KS2
SPELLING
SATs

WORKBOOK

JON GOULDING

About this book

Spelling

Learning to spell is an important stage in your child's education. It helps to develop key life skills, especially in reading, writing and languages.

This book is designed to help your child spell increasingly difficult words accurately, confidently and consistently. It will also aid preparation for the Key Stage 2 **English Grammar, Punctuation and Spelling** test.

Features of the book

- *Key to spelling* – explains each spelling concept with clear examples.

- *Practice activities* – a variety of tasks and questions to challenge your child.

- *Test your spelling* – enables your child to check their spelling of a particular group of words.

- *Test practice* – offers practice for the spelling task in the Key Stage 2 SATs.

- *Answers* are in a pull-out booklet at the centre of the book.

Spelling tips

- Ask your child to write a sentence which includes a particular word.

- Create flash cards – write problematic words on cards and display them as a visual reminder. Read words from the cards and ask your child to spell them.

- Make spelling fun – look for words on signs, etc., and encourage word play (e.g. how many words can you make from the word *supermarket*?).

ACKNOWLEDGEMENTS
The author and publisher are grateful to the copyright holders for permission to use quoted materials and images.
Cover, P01 ©Igorrita; P04 ©Matthew Cole; P06 ©Matthew Cole; P07 ©dedMazay; P08 ©RATOCA; P10 ©bigredlynx; P11 © Memo Angeles; P12 ©iralu; P14 ©Kheng Guan Toh, ©Barry Barnes; P16 ©Bradipoo; P17 ©Lorelyn Medina, © lineartestpilot; P18 ©Bueverova; P19 ©Klara Viskova; P20 ©Alexandra Petruk, © Matthew Cole; P22 ©Cory Thoman, ©Andre Adams; P24 ©Bobb Klissourski; P26 ©marina_ua, ©Memo Angeles; P28 ©mhatzapa; P29 ©HitToon.Com; P30 ©Fernando Jose V. Soares, ©Lorelyn Medina; P32 ©Avel Krieg, ©ayelet-keshet; P34 ©Bobb Klissourski, ©Memo Angeles; P36 ©Fejas, ©Marina Zakharova; P38 ©Gorelova, ©Lorelyn Medina, ©Bobb Klissourski, ©iaRada; P40 ©Jose Elias da Silva Neto; P48 ©Joennie Sindo; P48 ©Rozhkovs; P50 ©John T Takai;P 52 ©Anton Brand, P56 ©Dietmar Hoepfl, ©Lorelyn Medina; P57 ©cartoons; P68 ©TsipiLevin; P70 ©Ken Benner; P73 ©Andre Adams; P74 ©FotoYakov; p78 ©TRONIN ANDREI, ©Cory

Thoman; P80 ©John T Takai, ©Memo Angeles
The above images have been used under license from Shutterstock.com
P04 Clipart.com; P10 © Leckie & Leckie. Drawn by Pumpkin House; P40 ©Clipart,com; P48 © Leckie & Leckie. Drawn by Ellustration; P52 © Clipart. com, ©Hemera/Thinkstock
All other images are ©Jupiterimages or © Letts Educational, an imprint of HarperCollinsPublishers Ltd
Every effort has been made to trace copyright holders and obtain their permission for the use of copyright material. The author and publisher will gladly receive information enabling them to rectify any error or omission in subsequent editions. All facts are correct at time of going to press.
Published by Letts Educational
An imprint of HarperCollinsPublishers Ltd
1 London Bridge Street
London SE1 9GF
ISBN 9780008294182
First published 2013
This edition published 2018

10 9 8 7 6 5 4 3
Text and Design ©Letts Educational, an imprint of HarperCollinsPublishers Ltd
All rights reserved. No part of this publication may be reproduced, stored in a retrieval system, or transmitted, in any form or by any means, electronic, mechanical, photocopying, recording or otherwise, without the prior permission of Letts Educational.
British Library Cataloguing in Publication Data. A CIP record of this book is available from the British Library.
Commissioning Editor: Tammy Poggo
Author: Jon Goulding
Contributor: Louis Fidge
Project Manager: Richard Toms
Project Editor: Bruce Nicholson
Cover Design: Paul Oates
Inside Concept Design: Ian Wrigley
Layout: Jouve India Private Limited
Production: Natalia Rebow
Printed and bound by Martins the Printers, Berwick -upon-Tweed

Contents

Syllables	4	Unexpected vowel sounds	46
Suffixes	6	When i sounds like *ee*	48
Suffixing words ending in ce or ge	8	The consonant l	50
Suffixing words ending in y	10	The letter strings ci and ti	52
Prefixes	12	Unstressed vowels	54
Negative prefixes	14	Vowel endings other than e	56
Split long vowel sounds	16	Prefixes and meanings	58
Making words plural	18	Number prefixes	60
–cious and –tious endings	20	Anglo-Saxon prefixes	62
–cial and –tial endings	22	More Anglo-Saxon words	64
–ant and –ance endings	24	Anglo-Saxon suffixes	66
–ent and –ence endings	26	Latin words	68
Words ending in –able	28	Latin suffixes	70
Words ending in –ible	30	Greek words	72
Suffixing –fer words	32	French words	74
Using the hyphen to link words	34	The history of words	76
i before e except after c	36	Confusing words	78
The letter string ough	38	More confusing words	80
Silent letters	40	More words to practise	82
Words ending in –ate and –ite	42	Test practice	85
Singular and plural rule-breakers	44	Answers (centre pull-out)	1–8

Syllables

Key to spelling

When you say a word slowly, you can hear how many beats or **syllables** it has.

You can tap out the syllables of a word, as you say it, to help you spell it. Each syllable must contain at least one vowel.

joy	en - joy	en - joy - ment
This has **one** syllable.	This has **two** syllables.	This has **three** syllables.

Practice activities

1. Say each of the words slowly. Tap out the syllables. Write each word in the correct column of the table. There will be eight words in each column.

empty   spectacular   exterminate   hospital   introduce

letterbox   solid   convenient   careless   district

supersonic   arithmetic   chatterbox   inside   photography

finishing   tennis   information   supply   suspension

establish   helpful   attention   astonishment

two syllables	three syllables	four syllables
solid empty helpful tennis inside careless supply district 8	hospital finishing letterbox establish chatterbox attention introduce suspension 8	supersonic arithmetic spectacular exterminate convenient information astonishment photography 8

2. Complete the missing syllables in these three-syllable words. Write the whole word too.

a) dif + fer + _ent_ — different

b) in + _ter_ + est — interest

c) _es_ + tab + lish — establish

d) op + _po_ + site — opposite

e) _de_ + mol + ish — demolish

f) bi + cyc + _le_ — bicycle

g) vol + _ca_ + no — volcano

h) _lem_ + on + ade — lemonade

i) kid + _nap_ + per — kidnaper

j) sig + _nat_ + ure — signature

k) pun + _ish_ + ment — punishment

l) e + las + _tic_ — elastic

m) _de_ + ter + mine — determine

n) pro + _po_ + sal — proposal

o) tor + _na_ + do — tornado

p) _en_ + ter + tain — entertain

q) in + ven + _tion_ — invention

Test your spelling

Look at the words.

Say them aloud.

Cover the words.

Write them from memory.

Check your spelling.

encouragement ✓   exterminate ✓

sentimental ✓   interviewer ✓

hospital ✓   perimeter ✓

semicircle ✓   responsible ✓

concentration ✓   superhuman ✓

Suffixes

Key to spelling

Adding a **suffix** to a word can change the meaning or tense.

imagine	**imagined**	**imagination**
root word	past tense	noun
(a verb in this case)		

Practice activities

1. Change each of these verbs into nouns. The first one has been done for you.

   imagine   imagination   inform   information

   evaporate   evaporation   associate   association

   plant   plantation   exterminate   extermination

2. Change each of these nouns into verbs.

   creation   create   transportation   transport

   formation   formate   preparation   prepare

3. Write the rule for adding **–ion** or **–ation** to verbs ending in **–e** or **–ate**.

   Words like imagine lose the 'e' to gain the 'ation'. Words like exterminate lose the 'ate' to gain the 'ation'. Words like creation lose the 'ion' to gain an 'e' to become a verb again.

4. Look at the endings of the highlighted words in the sentences below. Notice that different endings give different meanings. Complete the sentences by underlining the correct word in bold.

a) The ~~music~~/**musician** played her violin.

b) All of the ~~inform~~/**information** was handed over to the police.

c) It was time to do some ~~revise~~/**revision** before the exam.

d) The wheel is probably the greatest **invention**/~~invent~~.

e) It was hard to ~~creation~~/**create** the magnificent cake.

f) They had great ~~admire~~/**admiration** for their mother.

g) There was a huge ~~explode~~/**explosion** in the factory.

h) It was hard to ~~division~~/**divide** the food equally.

i) The car almost had a ~~collide~~/**collision** in the snow.

j) The ~~electric~~/**electrician** fixed the washing machine.

k) It took a lot of **preparation**/~~prepare~~ to make the lunch.

l) It was an incredible **magic**/~~magician~~ trick.

Test your spelling

Look at the words.

Say them aloud.

Cover the words.

Write them from memory.

Check your spelling.

information ✓	sensation ✓	creation ✓
collision ✓	explosion ✓	musician ✓
preparation	division ✓	
electrician ✓	association ✓	

Suffixing words ending in ce or ge

Key to spelling

It can be tricky adding a suffix to words ending in **ce** or **ge**.

race + ing = racing

race + ed = raced

Rule 1

When adding a suffix beginning with **i** or **e**, after a word ending with **ce** or **ge**, you drop the **e**.

change + able = changeable

Rule 2

When adding a suffix beginning with **a** or **o**, after a word ending with **ce** or **ge**, you keep the **e**, so that the **c** and **g** are kept 'soft' sounding.

Practice activities

1. Complete this table by correctly adding the suffixes to the verbs.

   Use Rule 1 to help you.

verb	+ ing	+ ed
dance	dancing	danced
slice	slicing	sliced
bounce	bouncing	bounced
face	facing	faced
stage	staging	staged
force	forcing	forced
plunge	plunging	plunged

Suffixing words ending in ce or ge

2. Add the suffix **–able** to each verb to make it into an adjective.

Use Rule 2 to help you.

trace	~~traceabll~~ *traceable*	**service**	serviceable
charge	chargeable	**pronounce**	~~pronout~~ pronounceable
notice	noticeable	**manage**	manageable
replace	replaceable	**enforce**	enforceable

3. Add the suffix **–ous** to each noun to make it into an adjective.

courage	courageous	**outrage**	outrageous
advantage	advantageous		

4. Choose an adjective ending in **–able** and an adjective ending in **–ous** from your answers above. Use each of them correctly in a sentence of your own.

a) –able

I drew on my hand and it was not noticeable.

b) –ous

I felt courageous so I bunjee jumped.

Test your spelling

Look at the words.

Say them aloud.

Cover the words.

Write them from memory.

Check your spelling.

tracing ✓	glanced ✓	arranging ✓
hedged ✓	paging ✓	peaceable ✓
orangeade ✓	chargeable ✓	
courageous ✓	outrageous ✓	

Suffixing words ending in y

Key to spelling

You can avoid making spelling mistakes when adding suffixes to words ending in **y** by learning these rules.

play + ing = playing

play + er = player

Rule 1

When a word ends with a **vowel** + **y**, you can just add a suffix.

heavy + er = heavier

heavy + est = heaviest

Rule 2

When a word ends with a **consonant** + **y**, you usually change the **y** to **i** before adding a suffix.

Practice activities

1. Complete the table. The first one has been done for you.

    Use Rule 1 to help you.

word	+ ing	+ ed	+ s
play	playing	played	plays
delay			
sway			
annoy			
employ			
destroy			

2. Add the suffix to each root word. The first one has been done for you.

Use Rule 2 to help you.

baby + es ____babies____   copy + es _____

happy + ness _____   pity + ful _____

cry + ed _____   glory + ous _____

rely + able _____   rusty + er _____

pretty + est _____   fury + ous _____

3. Take the suffix off each word. Write the root word you are left with.

Use Rule 2 to help you.

berries _____   **smelliest** _____

tidily _____   **married** _____

luxurious _____   **emptiness** _____

carrier _____   **angrily** _____

Test your spelling

Look at the words.

Say them aloud.

Cover the words.

Write them from memory.

Check your spelling.

heaviness	readily	enviable
burial	glorious	applied
busier	happiest	
ladies	pitiful	

Prefixes

Key to spelling

Prefixes change the meaning of words. They are added in front of a root word.

market

root word

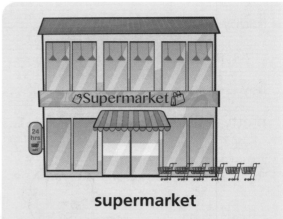

supermarket

new word with the prefix **super–**

Practice activities

1. Separate each of these words into the prefix and the root word. The first one has been done for you.

    a) disappear   dis   appear

    b) revisit   re   visit

    c) incomplete   in   complete

    d) superman   super   man

    e) international   inter   national

    f) mistrust   mis   trust

    g) submarine   sub   marine

    h) reheat   re   heat

2. Write down the meaning of the prefix used in the second word of each pair.

a) national; international

_____

b) clockwise; anticlockwise

_____

c) biography; autobiography

_____

3. Identify and underline the correct word in bold to use in each sentence.

a) The old car was a fine example of an early **mobile/~~automobile~~**.

b) First he made her disappear, then he made her **appear/~~reappear~~**.

c) He put cream on the wound to prevent it becoming **~~antiseptic~~/septic**.

d) The queen flew to several nations on her **national/~~international~~** trip.

4. Write the meaning of each of these prefixes.

a) re–visit

_____

b) sub–marine

_____

c) super–man

_____

Test your spelling

Look at the words.

Say them aloud.

Cover the words.

Write them from memory.

Check your spelling.

revisit	reinvent	submarine
international	supermarket	supercede
interrelate	anticlockwise	
automatic	automobile	

Negative prefixes

Adding a negative prefix to the beginning of a word gives the word the **opposite** meaning.

il + legal (prefix + root word)

= illegal (meaning 'not legal')

Practice activities

1. Add negative prefixes to the root words. Choose from **dis–**, **il–**, **im–**, **in–**, **ir–** and **un–**.

   _____cover   _____true

   _____legal   _____legible

   _____visible   _____active

   _____regular   _____relevant

   _____possible   _____patient

   _____honest   _____appear

2. Take the prefix off each word. Write the opposite of:

dishonest _____   impossible _____

illegible _____   uncover _____

untrue _____   impatient _____

3. Choose the correct prefix to add to each word to give it the opposite meaning.
Use a dictionary to help you.

un–   dis–   in–   im–   il–   ir–

_____approve   _____conscious

_____practical   _____definite

_____passive   _____literate

_____accurate   _____courteous

_____legal   _____relevant

_____reverent   _____discreet

_____necessary   _____movable

_____continue   _____logical

_____reparable   _____courage

_____pure   _____resistible

_____loyal   _____attentive

Test your spelling

Look at the words.

Say them aloud.

Cover the words.

Write them from memory.

Check your spelling.

unavailable	unknown	disloyal
disappear	invisible	inappropriate
immortal	impatient	
illegal	irregular	

Split long vowel sounds

Key to spelling

Sometimes a long vowel sound is split. This means the two vowels making the sound are separated by a consonant. The final vowel is an **e**.

Adding an **e** to the word **tap** creates a split long vowel sound, made by the **a** and the **e**, to give the word **tape**.

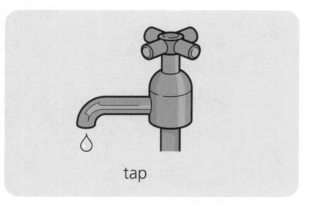

tap

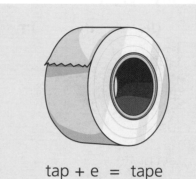

tap + e = tape

Practice activities

1. In each sentence there is a word which requires the addition of **e** to create a split long vowel sound. Write the new word. The first one has been done for you.

    a) The bed was mad.   _____made_____

    b) They tasted the win.   _____

    c) He made a not of the number.   _____

    d) They picked the rip fruit.   _____

    e) When the bus cam they were cold.   _____

    f) The superhero had a flowing cap.   _____

    g) Water was leaking from the pip.   _____

    h) Each dice was a cub shape.   _____

    i) She rod the horse for several miles.   _____

    j) It was peaceful in the dark pin forest.   _____

Split long vowel sounds

2. Add **–ing** to each of these words with split long vowel sounds.

ride	_____	shine	_____
come	_____	bite	_____
share	_____	hide	_____
smile	_____	face	_____

3. Write the rule for adding **–ing** to the words above.

_____

4. Change the following words to their past tense.

Be careful, some require changes within the word, not at the end.

note	_____	ride	_____
face	_____	hide	_____
come	_____	share	_____
shine	_____	smile	_____

Making words plural

Key to spelling

You just add **s** to many singular words to make them plural, e.g. one cat, two cat**s**. However, you need to learn the rules for the spelling of some other nouns.

one fox   two fox**es**

Rule 1

You add **es** to most nouns ending in **ch**, **sh**, **x** or **s** to make them plural.

one wolf   two wol**ves**

Rule 2

When a noun ends with **f** or **fe**, you usually change the **f** or **fe** to **v** and add **es** to make it plural.

Practice activities

1. Complete the table with the singular or plural forms of the nouns.

    Use Rule 1 to help you.

singular	plural
	dishes
address	
	watches
	wishes
church	
brush	
	arches
box	
	dashes

2. Write the plural of these words.

Use Rule 2 to help you.

loaf _____   thief _____

calf _____   knife _____

wolf _____   life _____

shelf _____   wife _____

3. Change each word to its plural form. The first one has been done for you.

half _____halves_____   hat _____

bus _____   holiday _____

tax _____   elf _____

branch _____   lion _____

benches	brushes	taxes
bosses	stitches	knives
loaves	shelves	
wolves	thieves	

–cious and –tious endings

Key to spelling

Very few common words end with **–cious** or **–tious**. They give a *shus* sound when added to a root word.

spa**ce** – spa**cious**

When the root word ends in **–ce**, the **ce** is dropped and **–cious** is added.

ficti**on** – ficti**tious**

Root words ending in other letters usually have **–tious** added.

Practice activities

1. Match up the pairs of words that contain the same root words. Underline the common root in both. The first one has been done for you.

    a) space ———————————— malicious

    b) caution —————— spacious

    c) grace   fictitious

    d) malice   vicious

    e) infect   gracious

    f) ambition   cautious

    g) vice   ambitious

    h) fiction   infectious

–cious and –tious endings

2. Fill in the white squares to complete the words.

m	a	l	i	c				s	
	m								
	b								
v	i			o	u	s		c	
								a	
f		c	t	i				u	s
								i	
	s							o	

3. Underline the correct word in bold to complete each sentence.

a) The book was a work of **fictitious/fiction**.

b) He prepared a very **nutrition/nutritious** meal.

c) They applauded and were **gracious/grace** in defeat.

d) The doctor wore a mask to prevent **infection/infectious**.

e) They were **suspicion/suspicious** of the stranger.

Test your spelling

Look at the words.

Say them aloud.

Cover the words.

Write them from memory.

Check your spelling.

vicious	precious	conscious
delicious	malicious	suspicious
ambitious	cautious	
infectious	nutritious	

–cial and –tial endings

Key to spelling

The word ending pronounced **shul** commonly uses **–cial** after a vowel and **–tial** after a consonant.

offi**cial**

TOP SECRET

confiden**tial**

There are exceptions which you have to learn. These include **initial**, **financial**, **commercial** and **provincial**.

Practice activities

1. Add the correct **–cial** or **–tial** ending to each word, writing the word in full.

    offi _____   confiden _____

    spe _____   artifi _____

    essen _____   par _____

2. Write a definition for each of the following words.

    Use a dictionary to help you.

    a) financial

    _____

    b) commercial

    _____

    c) provincial

    _____

3. Match the word families. The first one has been done for you.

a) confidential   office   financier

b) special   finance   confidence

c) official   part   speciality

d) financial   confident   partially

e) partial   specialise   officer

4. Write a sentence containing each given word.

a) artificial

_____

_____

b) essential

_____

_____

c) initial

_____

_____

Test your spelling

Look at the words.

Say them aloud.

Cover the words.

Write them from memory.

Check your spelling.

official	special	artificial
confidential	partial	essential
commercial	provincial	
financial	social	

–ant and –ance endings

Key to spelling

The **–ant** or **–ance** ending is often used if a word has a hard **c**, a hard **g** or when a related word has a long or short **a** sound near its end.

The man was hesit**ant**.

There was a moment of hesit**ance**.

The word hesit**a**tion has a long **a** sound.

Practice activities

1. Match the word families. The first one has been done for you.

   a) observant   hesitate   observance

   b) expectant   expectation   hesitation

   c) hesitant   observation   tolerance

   d) tolerant   substantial   expectancy

   e) substance   tolerate   substantially

2. Rewrite the list of words in alphabetical order.

   expectant   _____

   hesitant   _____

   substance   _____

   hesitance   _____

   expectance   _____

–ant and –ance endings

3. In the table below, replace the **–ant** endings with **–ancy** endings. One has been done for you.

–ant ending	–ancy ending
expectant	expectancy
hesitant	
flamboyant	
reluctant	

4. Complete the table with the correct **–ance** endings. One has been done for you.

–ancy ending	–ance ending
hesitancy	hesitance
reluctancy	
relevancy	
expectancy	

Test your spelling

Look at the words.

Say them aloud.

Cover the words.

Write them from memory.

Check your spelling.

observant	observance	expectant
hesitant	hesitance	substance
tolerant	tolerance	
relevant	relevance	

–ent and –ence endings

Key to spelling

The **–ent** or **–ence** ending is often used if a word has a soft **c**, a soft **g** or a **qu** sound, or when a related word has a clear **e** sound near the end.

intellig**ent**   intellig**ence**
soft **g**

innoc**ent**   innoc**ence**
soft **c**

Unfortunately, this is not a rule. There are many words which use **–ent** or **–ence**, but do not follow the above rule. You just have to learn them.

Practice activities

1. Match the word families. The first one has been done for you.

    a) innocent   decency   confidential

    b) decent   frequence   decently

    c) frequent   confidence   obediently

    d) confident   innocence   frequently

    e) obedient   obedience   innocently

2. Write the definition of each of these words.

    Use a dictionary to help you.

    a) confident

    _____

    b) obedient

    _____

    c) innocent

    _____

3. Complete the table with the correct **–ent** endings. One has been done for you.

–ence ending	–ent ending
innocence	innocent
frequence	
difference	
confidence	
independence	

4. Write a sentence containing each given word.

a) difference

_____

b) independent

_____

c) frequent

_____

d) confidence

_____

Test your spelling

Look at the words.

Say them aloud.

Cover the words.

Write them from memory.

Check your spelling.

innocent	innocence	independent
independence	obedient	obedience
confident	confidence	
different	difference	

Words ending in –able

Words which end in **–ation** can usually also end in **–able**. If a word ends in **ce** or **ge**, the **e** must be kept when adding **–able**.

ador**ation** – ador**able**

change**able**
(the root word ends in **ge**)

Practice activities

1. Match up the pairs of words that contain the same root words.

    a) adorable   notice

    b) noticeable   comfort

    c) changeable   consideration

    d) comfortable   adoration

    e) understandable   change

    f) reasonable   understand

    g) enjoyable   enjoy

    h) tolerable   toleration

    i) considerable   reason

2. Look at how the words below change when **–able** is added to the root word. In the space provided write a rule for what you see happening.

rely   ⟶   reli**able**

magnify   ⟶   magnifi**able**

_____

_____

3. Correctly add **–able** to the words below.

deny	_____	**comfort**	_____
notice	_____	**rectify**	_____
apply	_____	**adore**	_____
reason	_____	**vary**	_____
justify	_____	**enjoy**	_____

Test your spelling

Look at the words.

Say them aloud.

Cover the words.

Write them from memory.

Check your spelling.

adorable   considerable   noticeable

tolerable   reasonable   reliable

enjoyable   understandable

applicable   dependable

Words ending in –ible

Key to spelling

The **–ible** ending is often used if a complete root word cannot be heard before the ending.

horrid – horr**ible**

admit – admiss**ible**

There are plenty of exceptions to this rule, such as **sensible** and **forcible** (the words **sense** and **force** can be heard, even though the **e** is dropped).

Practice activities

1. Add the **–ible** ending to each of these words.

   force _____   collapse _____

   response _____   sense _____

2. Write the definition of each of these words.
   Use a dictionary to help you.

   a) edible

   _____

   b) audible

   _____

   c) visible

   _____

3. Fill in the white squares to complete the words.

	h	o	r	r						
			e					d		
v			s					i		t
i			p	o	s	s				
s								l		r
i			n					e		r
b			s							i
	e	g		b	l	e				b
			b							
			l							e
	c	r		d			l	e		

4. Write a sentence containing at least one of the **–ible** words from the word grid above.

_____

_____

Suffixing –fer words

Key to spelling

Words ending in **–fer** have two rules when adding suffixes which begin with vowels, e.g. **–er**, **–ing**, **–ence**.

infer – infe**rr**ed prefer – prefe**rr**ing The **r** is doubled if the **–fer** is stressed after the suffix has been added.	prefer – prefe**r**ence refer – refe**r**ence The **r** is not doubled if the **–fer** is not stressed after the suffix has been added.

Practice activities

1. Write out these words in the past tense by adding **–ed**. Decide whether you need to double the final **r**.

   prefer _____   **buffer** _____

   refer _____   **transfer** _____

   infer _____   **confer** _____

2. Underline the words which can have **–ing** added to them without doubling the **r**.

   transfer   **differ**

   occur   **offer**

   suffer   **prefer**

Suffixing –fer words

3. Write a sentence for each given word.

Use a dictionary to help you.

a) transferring

b) preferring

c) suffering

d) inferring

e) conferred

f) offered

g) reference

h) preference

i) referred

Test your spelling

Look at the words.

Say them aloud.

Cover the words.

Write them from memory.

Check your spelling.

referring	referral	preferring
preferred	transferred	transferring
suffered	preference	
offering	reference	

Using the hyphen to link words

Key to spelling

There are different views on the use of hyphens to link words. Often they are used to join a prefix to a root word.

co-ordinates

pre-owned

Notice that in the examples above, the prefix ends in a vowel and the root word begins with a vowel. This is a common use of the hyphen.

Practice activities

1. Write a sentence for each of these hyphenated words.

   Use a dictionary to help you become familiar with the meaning.

   a) co-own

   _____

   b) pre-eminent

   _____

   c) co-exist

   _____

   d) pre-owned

   _____

   e) co-ordinate

   _____

Using the hyphen to link words

2. Numbers and fractions which consist of two words are hyphenated, e.g. $\frac{3}{6}$ is written as three-sixths. Write the following in full.

$\frac{3}{4}$ _____   48 _____

92 _____ $\frac{2}{3}$ _____

37 _____ $\frac{3}{5}$ _____

$\frac{8}{10}$ _____   84 _____

$\frac{5}{6}$ _____   59 _____

3. The prefixes **self–**, **ex–** and **cross–** are followed by a hyphen before the root word is added. Choose the correct prefix for the words below, then write the hyphenated word in full.

a) country _____

b) discipline _____

c) wife _____

d) policeman _____

e) training _____

f) aware _____

Test your spelling

Look at the words.

Say them aloud.

Cover the words.

Write them from memory.

Check your spelling.

re-iterate   pre-eminent   co-own

pre-owned   re-invent   re-apply

co-exist   co-ordinate

middle-aged   self-discipline

i before e except after c

Key to spelling

The **i** before **e** except after **c** rule applies when the sound represented is **ee**, as in p**ee**p. Therefore, science and efficient do not follow the rule.

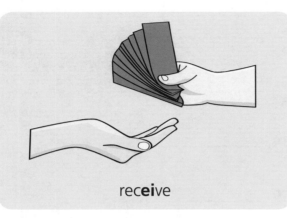

rec**ei**ve

c**ei**ling

There are, however, many exceptions to the rule when the **ei** is present without following **c**.

Practice activities

1. Complete the table with the words from the list below.

deceive	perceive	protein	receive
conceive	caffeine	receipt	ceiling
deceit	conceit	seize	weird

ei after c	ei exceptions

2. Complete and write in full these **ei** or **ie** words.

Use a dictionary to help if you are unsure.

th_____f _____

bel_____ve _____

c_____ling _____

ch_____f _____

ach_____ve _____

rec_____ve _____

s_____ze _____

p_____ce _____

dec_____ve _____

caff_____ne _____

3. Write a sentence for each of the following words.

a) achieve

_____

b) receive

_____

c) deceive

_____

d) weird

_____

e) seize

_____

Test your spelling

Look at the words.

Say them aloud.

Cover the words.

Write them from memory.

Check your spelling.

ceiling	conceive	caffeine
perceive	achieve	receive
protein	seize	
conceit	deceive	

The letter string ough

The letter string **ough** is one of the trickiest spelling patterns in English because **ough** is used to represent several different sounds.

or sound (as in f**or**d)	*u* sound (as in c**u**t)	*o* sound (as in t**o**p)	*o* sound (as in n**o**)

th**ough**t	r**ough**	c**ough**	d**ough**

Practice activities

1. Rewrite the list of **ough** words in alphabetical order.

   although _____

   tough _____

   dough _____

   bought _____

   nought _____

   enough _____

   cough _____

   though _____

   rough _____

   brought _____

2. Look at the following **ough** words. Match each **ough** word to the word which contains a sound closest to the **ough** sound being used. The first one has been done for you.

a) borough   cow

b) through   horror

c) enough   blow

d) plough   blue

e) although   lord

f) bought   huff

3. Write a definition for each of the following words.

Use a dictionary to help you.

a) borough

_____

b) through

_____

c) thorough

_____

d) bought

_____

Test your spelling

Look at the words.

Say them aloud.

Cover the words.

Write them from memory.

Check your spelling.

ought	bought	nought
thought	though	through
plough	thorough	
enough	although	

Silent letters

Key to spelling

Some words contain **silent letters**. In the past these letters were often pronounced, but now you cannot hear the letters when you say the words. Here are examples of the silent **g**, **k** and **w** in use:

You **g**nash your teeth.

You tie a **k**not.

You **w**rite a letter.

Practice activities

1. Fill in the missing silent **g**, **k** or **w**. The first one has been done for you.
    Use a dictionary if necessary.

    k̲now   __not   __rap

    __nash   __naw   __rite

    __rong   __riggle   __reck

    __nome   __nit   __nat

    __narled   __nee   __ren

2. Underline the silent letter in each of these words. The first one has been done for you.

a<u>i</u>sle	island	lamb
gnome	doubt	debris
thistle	solemn	walk
thumb	dumb	talk

3. Fill in the missing letter in each rule.

Rule 1

A silent **g** at the beginning of a word is always followed by the letter __.

Rule 2

A silent **k** at the beginning of a word is always followed by the letter __.

Rule 3

A silent **w** at the beginning of a word is always followed by the letter __.

Rule 4

A silent **b** in a word often comes after the letter __.

Rule 5

A silent **t** in a word often comes before the letter __.

Test your spelling

Look at the words.

Say them aloud.

Cover the words.

Write them from memory.

Check your spelling.

knight	thistle	solemn
lamb	island	doubt
gnome	wrong	
castle	walk	

Words ending in –ate and –ite

The endings **–ate** and **–ite** are quite common.

The pir**ate** was not very pol**ite**!

You have to learn which ending to use.

Practice activities

1. Write out these in full with the correct ending, **–ate** or **–ite**. The first one has been done for you.

    Use a dictionary to help you.

priv	private	**rec**	_____
favour	_____	**decor**	_____
inv	_____	**chocol**	_____
consider	_____	**defin**	_____
ign	_____	**clim**	_____

2. Write a sentence containing the pair of words given to you.

    a) favourite   chocolate

    _____

    b) decorate   private

    _____

Words ending in –ate and –ite

3. Write the complete versions of each of these in the table below. The completed words should end in **–ate** or **–ite**.

investig	exc	exquis
desper	fortun	irrit
dynam	oppos	favour
defin	infl	illustr
separ	pol	appet

–ate words	–ite words

Test your spelling

Look at the words.

Say them aloud.

Cover the words.

Write them from memory.

Check your spelling.

create	educate	deliberate
polite	certificate	ignite
definite	demonstrate	
opposite	favourite	

Singular and plural rule-breakers

Key to spelling

The spelling of most nouns follow simple rules when you write their plural forms. However, some nouns do not stick to the rules!

You can say:

one house and two house**s**

However, you should not say:

one mouse and two mouses

Practice activities

1. Match up the singular and plural forms of these nouns. Some words have the same singular and plural form. Match these and underline them. The first one has been done for you.

singular	plural	singular	plural
mouse	teeth	child	deer
goose	feet	person	people
man	mice	louse	fish
tooth	oxen	sheep	women
ox	aircraft	fish	lice
aircraft	men	deer	sheep
foot	geese	woman	children

Answers

Pages 4–5

1.

two syllables	three syllables	four syllables
empty	hospital	spectacular
solid	introduce	exterminate
careless	letterbox	convenient
district	chatterbox	supersonic
inside	finishing	arithmetic
tennis	suspension	photography
supply	establish	information
helpful	attention	astonishment

2. **a)** differ**ent** **b)** in**ter**est **c) es**tablish
    d) op**po**site **e)** de**mo**lish **f)** bicy**cle**
    g) vol**ca**no **h)** lem**o**nade **i)** kid**nap**per
    j) sig**nat**ure **k)** pun**ish**ment **l)** elas**tic**
    m) de**po**sal **n)** pro**po**sal
    o) tor**pe**do/tor**na**do **p) en**tertain
    q) inven**tion**/inven**tor**

Pages 6–7

1. imagination, information, evaporation, association, plantation, extermination
2. create, transport, form, prepare
3. If the verb ends in **–e**, drop the **e** and add **–ation**. If the verb ends in **–ate**, drop the **e** and add **–ion**.
4. **a)** musician **b)** information **c)** revision
    d) invention **e)** create **f)** admiration
    g) explosion **h)** divide **i)** collision
    j) electrician **k)** preparation **l)** magic

Pages 8–9

1. dance/dancing/danced; slice/slicing/sliced; bounce/bouncing/bounced; face/facing/faced; stage/staging/staged; force/forcing/forced; plunge/plunging/plunged
2. traceable, serviceable, chargeable, pronounceable, noticeable, manageable, replaceable, enforceable
3. courageous, outrageous, advantageous
4. **a)–b)** Sentences will vary, but they must contain the stated word with the correct spelling, must be correctly punctuated and must make sense.

Pages 10–11

1. playing/played/plays; delaying/delayed/delays; swaying/swayed/sways; annoying/annoyed/annoys; employing/employed/employs; destroying/destroyed/destroys
2. babies, copies, happiness, pitiful, cried, glorious, reliable, rustier, prettiest, furious
3. berry, smelly, tidy, marry, luxury, empty, carry, angry

Pages 12–13

1. **a)** dis; appear **b)** re; visit **c)** in; complete
    d) super; man **e)** inter; national
    f) mis; trust **g)** sub; marine **h)** re; heat
2. **a)** inter– means 'between' or 'among'
    b) anti– means 'against'
    c) auto– means 'self' or 'own'
3. **a)** automobile **b)** reappear **c)** septic
    d) international
4. **a)** re– means 'again' or 'back'
    b) sub– means 'under'
    c) super– means 'above'

Pages 14–15

1. uncover, untrue, illegal, illegible, invisible, inactive, irregular, irrelevant, impossible, impatient, dishonest, disappear
2. honest, possible, legible, cover, true, patient
3. disapprove, unconscious, impractical, indefinite, impassive, illiterate, inaccurate, discourteous, illegal, irrelevant, irreverent, indiscreet, unnecessary, immovable, discontinue, illogical, irreparable, discourage, impure, irresistible, disloyal, inattentive

Pages 16–17

1. **a)** made **b)** wine **c)** note **d)** ripe
    e) came **f)** cape **g)** pipe **h)** cube
    i) rode **j)** pine
2. riding, shining, coming, biting, sharing, hiding, smiling, facing
3. Drop the **e** before adding **–ing**.
4. noted, rode, faced, hid, came, shared, shone, smiled

Answers

Pages 18–19

1. dish/dishes; address/addresses; watch/watches; wish/wishes; church/churches; brush/brushes; arch/arches; box/boxes; dash/dashes

2. loaves, thieves, calves, knives, wolves, lives, shelves, wives

3. halves, hats, buses, holidays, taxes, elves, branches, lions

Pages 20–21

1. a) space/spacious b) caution/cautious c) grace/gracious d) malice/malicious e) infect/infectious f) ambition/ambitious g) vice/vicious h) fiction/fictitious

2. **Across:** malicious, vicious, fictitious
   Down: ambitious, cautious

3. a) fiction b) nutritious c) gracious d) infection e) suspicious

Pages 22–23

1. official, confidential, special, artificial, essential, partial

2. a) financial – related to money and finance
   b) commercial – related to commerce and business
   c) provincial – local or related to a province

3. a) confidential/confident/confidence b) special/specialise/speciality c) official/office/officer d) financial/finance/financier e) partial/part/partially

4. a)–c) Sentences will vary, but they must contain the stated word with the correct spelling, must be correctly punctuated and must make sense.

Pages 24–25

1. a) observant/observation/observance
   b) expectant/expectation/expectancy
   c) hesitant/hesitate/hesitation
   d) tolerant/tolerate/tolerance
   e) substance/substantial/substantially

2. expectance, expectant, hesitance, hesitant, substance

3. expectant/expectancy; hesitant/hesitancy; flamboyant/flamboyancy; reluctant/reluctancy

4. hesitancy/hesitance; reluctancy/reluctance; relevancy/relevance; expectancy/expectance

Pages 26–27

1. a) innocent/innocence/innocently
   b) decent/decency/decently c) frequent/frequence/frequently d) confident/confidence/confidential e) obedient/obedience/obediently

2. a) confident – having a strong belief that something will happen
   b) obedient – obeying an order or wish directed at you
   c) innocent – having done nothing wrong

3. innocence/innocent; frequence/frequent; difference/different; confidence/confident; independence/independent

4. a)–d) Sentences will vary, but they must contain the stated word with the correct spelling, must be correctly punctuated and must make sense.

Pages 28–29

1. a) adorable/adoration b) noticeable/notice c) changeable/change d) comfortable/comfort e) understandable/understand f) reasonable/reason g) enjoyable/enjoy h) tolerable/toleration i) considerable/consideration

2. The **y** is replaced by **i** before adding **–able**.

3. deniable, comfortable, noticeable, rectifiable, applicable, adorable, reasonable, variable, justifiable, enjoyable

Pages 30–31

1. forcible, collapsible, responsible, sensible

2. a) edible – something which can be eaten
   b) audible – something which can be heard
   c) visible – something which can be seen

3. **Across:** horrible, possible, legible, credible
   Down: visible, responsible, edible, terrible

Answers

4. Sentences will vary, but they must contain at least one word from activity 3 with the correct spelling, must be correctly punctuated and must make sense.

Pages 32–33

1. preferred, buffered, referred, transferred, inferred, conferred

2. differ, offer, suffer

3. a)–i) Sentences will vary, but they must contain the stated word with the correct spelling, must be correctly punctuated and must make sense.

Pages 34–35

1. a)–e) Sentences will vary, but they must contain the stated word with the correct spelling, must be correctly punctuated and must make sense.

2. three-quarters, forty-eight, ninety-two, two-thirds, thirty-seven, three-fifths, eight-tenths, eighty-four, five-sixths, fifty-nine

3. a) cross-country b) self-discipline
c) ex-wife d) ex-policeman
e) cross-training f) self-aware

Pages 36–37

1.

ei after c	ei exceptions
deceive, perceive, receive, conceive, receipt, ceiling, deceit, conceit	protein, caffeine, seize, weird

2. th**ie**f, rec**ei**ve, bel**ie**ve, s**ei**ze, c**ei**ling, p**ie**ce, ch**ie**f, dec**ei**ve, ach**ie**ve, caff**ei**ne

3. a)–e) Sentences will vary, but they must contain the stated word with the correct spelling, must be correctly punctuated and must make sense.

Pages 38–39

1. although, bought, brought, cough, dough, enough, nought, rough, though, tough

2. a) borough/horror b) through/blue
c) enough/huff d) plough/cow
e) although/blow f) bought/lord

3. a) borough – an area of a city
b) through – when something goes in one way and out another
c) thorough – when something is done completely
d) bought – to get something in return for payment

Pages 40–41

1. know, knot, wrap, gnash, gnaw, write, wrong, wriggle, wreck, gnome, knit, gnat, gnarled, knee, wren

2. aisle, island, lamb, gnome, doubt, debris, thistle, solemn, walk, thumb, dumb, talk

3. **Rule 1** – n, **Rule 2** – n, **Rule 3** – r, **Rule 4** – m, **Rule 5** – l

Pages 42–43

1. private, recite, favourite, decorate, invite, chocolate, considerate, definite, ignite, climate

2. a)–b) Sentences will vary, but they must contain the stated words with the correct spelling, must be correctly punctuated and must make sense.

3. –ate words: investigate, desperate, fortunate, irritate, inflate, illustrate, separate
–ite words: excite, exquisite, dynamite, opposite, favourite, definite, polite, appetite

Pages 44–45

1. mouse/mice; goose/geese; man/men; tooth/teeth; ox/oxen; aircraft/aircraft; foot/feet; child/children; person/people; louse/lice; sheep/sheep; fish/fish; deer/deer; woman/women

2. a)–e) Sentences will vary, but they must include *women*, *mice*, *children*, *sheep* and *people* with the correct spelling, must be correctly punctuated and must make sense.

3. cacti/cactuses, oases, media, gateaux, formulae, fungi, larvae, radiuses/radii, plateaux, crises

3

Answers

Pages 46–47

1. none, nothing, love, above, son, shove, among, month, front, dozen, wonder, money, monkey, sponge, accomplish
2. double, trouble, couple, touch, young, country
3. wash, wand, warrant, waddle, swamp, swallow, wallow, wallet, wasp, watch
4. Answers could include: wash, wasp, watch; glove, nothing, month

Pages 48–49

1. i comes before a: brilliant, immediate, familiar, radiant, material, memorial
   i comes before e: alien, premier, experience, obedient, convenient
   i comes before o: companion, opinion, warrior, mysterious
2. a) warrior b) brilliant c) familiar
   d) premier e) opinion f) companion
   g) radiant h) convenient i) immediate
   j) mysterious k) obedient l) alien
   m) material n) experience o) memorial

Pages 50–51

1. a) call b) hall c) ball d) well e) sell
   f) tell g) mill h) pill i) doll j) pull k) full
2. always, almost, alone, already, although, almighty
3. comic, season, nation, music, region, topic, tropic, logic
4. useful, hopeful, powerful, cheerful, helpful, painful, restful, thankful

Pages 52–53

1. ci: special, musician, ancient, suspicion, delicious
   ti: patient, initial, essential, infectious, cautious
2. a) musician b) essential c) delicious
   d) suspicion e) patient f) cautious
   g) special
3. a)–h) Sentences will vary, but they must contain the stated word with the correct spelling, must be correctly punctuated and must make sense.

Pages 54–55

1. vegetables, camera, diamond, different, interest, history, separate, mathematics, mystery, valuable, company, temperature
2. dangerous, Wednesday, January, marvellous, fastener, delivery, jewellery, freedom, company, business, Saturday, February, generous, gardener, mineral, factory, century, necessary, animal, separate, interest, history, voluntary, offering

Pages 56–57

1. words ending with a: pizza, opera, pasta
   words ending with i: spaghetti, ravioli, macaroni
   words ending with o: solo, cello, piano, risotto
2. anaconda, bongo, chapatti, kimono, gnu, gecko, kiwi, banana, radio/radii, armadillo, dingo, camera, puma, samosa, bhaji, emu, sofa, tarantula

Pages 58–59

1. a) subway, telephone, television, submarine
   b) transfer, autobiography, translate, autograph c) surface, surplus, circumstances, circumference
2. a) submarine b) subway
3. a) television b) telephone
4. a) autobiography b) translate c) autograph
   d) transfer
5. a) circumstances b) surface c) surplus
   d) circumference

Pages 60–61

1. tricycle, unicycle, bicycle
2. a) unicorn – a mythical white horse with one horn
   b) unison – everyone singing the same one note
   c) unify – to make into one
   d) unique – the only one of its kind
3. a) bisect b) bilingual c) biped
   d) bicycle
4. a) triple b) triangle c) trio d) tricycle

Pages 62–63

1. a) begrudge b) bewitch c) mismanage
    d) misspell e) misuse f) becalm
2. a) becalm b) mismanage c) misuse
    d) misspell
3. Answers will vary, but could include:
    ashore, foretell, offshoot, outlive,
    overreach, undone, withhold

Pages 64–65

1. **Family words:** moder/mother; faeder/
    father; sweoster/sister; brothor/brother;
    sunu/son; dohter/daughter
    Colour words: blew/blue; read/red; hwit/
    white; brun/brown; silfer/silver; geolo/
    yellow
2. a) hors/horse b) gat/cat c) docga/dog
    d) wulf/wolf e) sceap/sheep
3. a) floetan/fleet b) sceran/scrape
    c) faran/far d) beran/barrow e) wegan/
    wagon f) laeran/learn g) witan/wisdom

Pages 66–67

1. **–en:** quicken, soften, brighten, lighten
    –er: boxer, printer, teacher, gardener
2. fat, shave, white, worry
3. witchcraft/woodcraft; northern/eastern;
    wholesome/tiresome; playwright/
    wheelwright; backward/homeward;
    artful/merciful; warlike/lifelike; lengthwise/
    otherwise; childish/foolish

Pages 68–69

1. primary, aeroplane, aquarium, audience,
    subway, expel, conjunction, supersonic
2. a) amo/amiable b) corpus/corpse
    c) dentis/dental d) moveo/movement
    e) pendeo/pendulum f) tempus/temporary
    g) sedeo/reside h) caput/captain i) curro/
    current j) manus/manufacture k) poena/
    penalty l) verbum/proverb

Pages 70–71

1. fashionable, invisible, responsible, suitable,
    reasonable, remarkable, horrible, flexible
2. value, rely, deplore, move, memory, use

3. a) leak b) assist c) giant d) mountain
    e) family f) sign g) just h) rely
    Sentences will vary, but they must contain
    the stated word with the correct spelling,
    must be correctly punctuated and must
    make sense.

Pages 72–73

1. Answers will vary, but they could
    include: antiseptic, archbishop,
    autograph, parallel, telephone,
    microphone, photograph, diameter
2. a) aster/astrology b) grapho/autograph
    c) logos/dialogue d) pathos/pathetic
    e) polis/politics f) gramma/grammar
    g) sphaira/sphere h) bios/biology
    i) kosmos/cosmetic j) metron/metre
    k) phone/microphone l) skopeo/telescope
    m) oide/melody n) optikus/optician

Pages 74–75

1. duvet, trumpet, cricket, cabaret, ballet,
    scarlet, bracket, bouquet, ticket, buffet
2. *ay* sound: duvet, cabaret, ballet, bouquet,
    buffet
    et sound: trumpet, cricket, scarlet, bracket,
    ticket
3. a) ballet b) cabaret c) duvet
4. a)–e) Sentences will vary, but they must
    contain the stated word with the
    correct spelling, must be correctly
    punctuated and must make sense.

Pages 76–77

1. a) Tuesday b) Friday c) Thursday
    d) Sunday e) Saturday f) Monday
2. a) August b) May c) January d) July
    e) June
3. a) September b) October c) November
    d) December
4. a) biro – a ballpoint pen. Named after the
    inventor of the ballpoint pen, Laszlo
    Biro.
    b) diesel – a type of fuel. Named after
    Rudolf Diesel, who invented the diesel
    engine.

Answers

c) pasteurise – a process to prolong the life of food. Named after Louis Pasteur, the French microbiologist.

Pages 78–79

1. **a)** advise **b)** devise **c)** license **d)** practise
   Sentences will vary, but they must contain the verb or noun with the correct spelling, must be correctly punctuated and must make sense.

2. **a)** heard – past tense of the verb hear
   b) herd – a group of animals
   c) ascent – the act of ascending (going up)
   d) assent – to agree/agreement
   e) profit – money made in selling things
   f) prophet – someone who foretells the future
   g) aisle – a passageway between seats
   h) isle – an island
   i) farther – further
   j) father – a male parent

Pages 80–81

1. **a)** affect – usually a verb, e.g. the weather will **affect** the race; effect – usually a noun, e.g. it could have an **effect** on the race.
   b) desert – a barren place; dessert – a sweet course after the main course of a meal
   c) eligible – suitable to be chosen or elected; illegible – not legible
   d) guest – somebody receiving hospitality; guessed – past tense of the verb guess

2. who's/whose; aloud/allowed; altar/ alter; bridal/bridle; cereal/serial; led/lead; compliment/complement; steal/steel; stationary/stationery; descent/dissent

3. Sentences will vary, but they must contain the stated words with the correct spelling, must be correctly punctuated and must make sense.

Pages 85–88

Note to parent: For each test, read the word, then the word within a sentence, then repeat the word a third time. You should leave at least a 12-second gap between spellings.

Test 1

1. The word is **sprint**. She can **sprint** very fast. The word is **sprint**.
2. The word is **knew**. They **knew** that the sea was cold. The word is **knew**.
3. The word is **something**. I think I can see **something** under the tree. The word is **something**.
4. The word is **station**. The lost keys were at the police **station**. The word is **station**.
5. The word is **difficult**. He found the maths test **difficult**. The word is **difficult**.
6. The word is **earn**. I **earn** pocket money cleaning the car. The word is **earn**.
7. The word is **ambitious**. She is so **ambitious**. The word is **ambitious**.
8. The word is **allowed**. Dogs are not **allowed** in the shop. The word is **allowed**.
9. The word is **opinion**. In my **opinion** they are silly. The word is **opinion**.
10. The word is **convince**. I will **convince** you to join our club. The word is **convince**.

Test 2

1. The word is **gather**. Please help me to **gather** the wood. The word is **gather**.
2. The word is **wonderful**. It is really **wonderful** to see you again. The word is **wonderful**.
3. The word is **when**. I will do it **when** I return. The word is **when**.
4. The word is **pleasure**. They took so much **pleasure** from the letter. The word is **pleasure**.
5. The word is **disturb**. Be quiet so you do not **disturb** the baby. The word is **disturb**.
6. The word is **grammar**. Her ideas are good, but her **grammar** lets her down. The word is **grammar**.
7. The word is **library**. I must return the book to the **library**. The word is **library**.

Answers

8. The word is **cautious**. It pays to be **cautious** when walking on ice. The word is **cautious**.

9. The word is **exterminate**. The pest control officer was called to **exterminate** the rats. The word is **exterminate**.

10. The word is **yacht**. A lovely **yacht** sailed past the beach. The word is **yacht**.

Test 3

1. The word is **healthy**. **Healthy** food is excellent. The word is **healthy**.

2. The word is **people**. I need to know which **people** to call. The word is **people**.

3. The word is **room**. Please leave the bag in my **room**. The word is **room**.

4. The word is **beginning**. Let's start at the very **beginning**. The word is **beginning**.

5. The word is **typical**. It was a **typical** wet day. The word is **typical**.

6. The word is **early**. I woke up too **early** today. The word is **early**.

7. The word is **immediate**. We need **immediate** help. The word is **immediate**.

8. The word is **fictitious**. The whole story was **fictitious**. The word is **fictitious**.

9. The word is **special**. There was a **special** gift awaiting them. The word is **special**.

10. The word is **estimate**. They could only **estimate** how long it would take. The word is **estimate**.

Test 4

1. The word is **museum**. Do not walk through the **museum**. The word is **museum**.

2. The word is **love**. We **love** to lie on the beach. The word is **love**.

3. The word is **there**. **There** is a great film showing tonight. The word is **there**.

4. The word is **different**. I have a **different** idea than you. The word is **different**.

5. The word is **happily**. The day ended **happily** for all involved. The word is **happily**.

6. The word is **disguise**. The robber had a cunning **disguise**. The word is **disguise**.

7. The word is **excite**. Showing them the tickets is sure to **excite** them. The word is **excite**.

8. The word is **infectious**. Keep away from others as you are still **infectious**. The word is **infectious**.

9. The word is **hinder**. Please do not **hinder** our progress. The word is **hinder**.

10. The word is **theatre**. Let's go to the **theatre** tonight. The word is **theatre**.

Test 5

1. The word is **step**. Make sure you do not **step** on the cracks. The word is **step**.

2. The word is **their**. It will be **their** own fault if they miss the bus. The word is **their**.

3. The word is **hope**. We can only **hope** we get there on time. The word is **hope**.

4. The word is **measure**. **Measure** the width of the window carefully. The word is **measure**.

5. The word is **national**. There was a **national** shortage of petrol. The word is **national**.

6. The word is **madness**. It is **madness** to think you can jump over that. The word is **madness**.

7. The word is **because**. I will be back **because** I need to collect my things. The word is **because**.

8. The word is **forgotten**. He did not want to be **forgotten** by the others. The word is **forgotten**.

9. The word is **experience**. The parachute jump was a great **experience**. The word is **experience**.

10. The word is **improve**. We must **improve** our shooting and passing. The word is **improve**.

11. The word is **increase**. If you cannot hear, just **increase** the volume. The word is **increase**.

Answers

12. The word is **thought**. I **thought** we would be there by now. The word is **thought**.
13. The word is **reasonable**. It is a **reasonable** sum of money to share. The word is **reasonable**.
14. The word is **preferred**. They **preferred** to go swimming. The word is **preferred**.
15. The word is **precious**. The necklace had a very **precious** diamond pendant. The word is **precious**.
16. The word is **sensible**. Everyone was being very **sensible** in the line. The word is **sensible**.
17. The word is **popular**. Cycling is very **popular** in the summer months. The word is **popular**.
18. The word is **correspond**. We can **correspond** with each other by email. The word is **correspond**.
19. The word is **yeast**. **Yeast** is used to make bread rise. The word is **yeast**.
20. The word is **curious**. There was a very **curious** incident at lunchtime. The word is **curious**.

Test 6
1. The word is **make**. Let's **make** some cakes. The word is **make**.
2. The word is **sea**. They all went to look at the **sea**. The word is **sea**.
3. The word is **door**. Open the **door** to let the cat out. The word is **door**.
4. The word is **international**. The pop group were **international** superstars. The word is **international**.
5. The word is **relative**. The new boy in Year 1 has a **relative** in Year 3. The word is **relative**.
6. The word is **interest**. They always show great **interest** in the chocolate cakes. The word is **interest**.
7. The word is **explore**. The first thing we will do is **explore** the area. The word is **explore**.

8. The word is **machine**. It was an incredible flying **machine**. The word is **machine**.
9. The word is **famous**. When I grow up, I might be **famous**. The word is **famous**.
10. The word is **hesitant**. She was very **hesitant** about going to her new school. The word is **hesitant**.
11. The word is **vicious**. A **vicious** looking dog snarled from behind the fence. The word is **vicious**.
12. The word is **through**. Let everyone **through** so they can get to assembly. The word is **through**.
13. The word is **although**. **Although** it was raining, they still had great fun. The word is **although**.
14. The word is **decent**. The book was in **decent** condition. The word is **decent**.
15. The word is **ceiling**. The decorator stood on a ladder to paint the **ceiling**. The word is **ceiling**.
16. The word is **delicious**. The chef created a **delicious** meal. The word is **delicious**.
17. The word is **preference**. It was her **preference** to walk to school. The word is **preference**.
18. The word is **privilege**. It is a great **privilege** to meet the Queen. The word is **privilege**.
19. The word is **mosquito**. I could hear the **mosquito** buzzing around the room. The word is **mosquito**.
20. The word is **Europe**. Britain is an island in northern **Europe**. The word is **Europe**.

Singular and plural rule-breakers

2. Write sentences containing the plural form of the given words.

a) woman

_____

b) mouse

_____

c) child

_____

d) sheep

_____

e) person

_____

3. Write the plural form of each of these words.

Use a dictionary to help you.

cactus	_____	**oasis**	_____
medium	_____	**gateau**	_____
formula	_____	**fungus**	_____
larva	_____	**radius**	_____
plateau	_____	**crisis**	_____

Test your spelling

Look at the words.

Say them aloud.

Cover the words.

Write them from memory.

Check your spelling.

mouse	mice	person
people	child	children
goose	geese	
fungus	fungi	

Unexpected vowel sounds

Key to spelling

Some vowels do not always behave in the way you expect them to.

glove

In some words the
letter **o** sounds like **u**.

wash

In some words the
letter **a** sounds like **o**.

Practice activities

1. Add the missing **o** to each of these words.

   *Say each word aloud and listen to the sound the **o** makes.*

n__ne	n__thing	l__ve
ab__ve	s__n	sh__ve
am__ng	m__nth	fr__nt
d__zen	w__nder	m__ney
m__nkey	sp__nge	acc__mplish

2. Add the missing **ou** to each of these words.

   *Say each word aloud and listen to the sound the **ou** makes.*

d_____ble	tr_____ble	c_____ple
t_____ch	y_____ng	c_____ntry

Unexpected vowel sounds

3. These words have been spelt as they sound, using an **o** to make the **o** sound, as in n**o**t. However, the words have been spelt incorrectly with the **o** included. Rewrite them correctly, replacing the incorrect **o** in each.

wosh _____   **wond** _____

worrant _____   **woddle** _____

swomp _____   **swollow** _____

wollow _____   **wollet** _____

wosp _____   **wotch** _____

4. Write three examples of words in which the letter **a** makes an **o** sound, as in n**o**t, and three examples of words where the letter **o** makes a **u** sound, as in p**u**t.

_____   _____   _____

_____   _____   _____

Test your spelling

Look at the words.

Say them aloud.

Cover the words.

Write them from memory.

Check your spelling.

front	nothing	above
month	double	swamp
touch	wander	
wallet	accomplish	

47

When i sounds like ee

Key to spelling

When **i** comes before a vowel, it often sounds like **ee**.

champion

barrier

radio

Practice activities

1. In the words below, the **i** makes an **ee** sound. Copy the words into the correct column in the table.

alien	brilliant	immediate	companion	premier
familiar	opinion	experience	radiant	obedient
material	warrior	mysterious	memorial	convenient

words in which:		
i comes before a	i comes before e	i comes before o

48

2. Look at the words from practice activity 1. Decide which word matches each definition below.

Use a dictionary to help you.

a) someone who fights in wars   _____

b) fantastic   _____

c) well known to you   _____

d) first or chief   _____

e) something you believe   _____

f) a friend   _____

g) giving off heat or light   _____

h) handy or easy to use   _____

i) straight away   _____

j) strange   _____

k) willing to do what you are told   _____

l) something which does not belong   _____

m) what garments are made from   _____

n) to find out what something is like   _____

o) a place to remember someone   _____

Test your spelling

Look at the words.

Say them aloud.

Cover the words.

Write them from memory.

Check your spelling.

million	studio	familiar
carrier	senior	audience
brilliant	immediate	
curious	convenient	

The consonant l

Key to spelling

Rule 1

At the end of words of one syllable, you double the **l**.

fall

Rule 2

When you add **–full**, **–all** or **all–** to a word, you drop one **l**.

Always be careful not to have an accidental fall!

all + ways = always

care + full = careful

accident + all = accidental

Practice activities

1. Add the correct **l** ending to each of these, then write the word correctly in full. They are all single-syllable words.

    a) ca_____   _____

    b) ha_____   _____

    c) ba_____   _____

    d) we_____   _____

    e) se_____   _____

    f) te_____   _____

    g) mi_____   _____

    h) pi_____   _____

    i) do_____   _____

    j) pu_____   _____

    k) fu_____   _____

2. Rewrite each word correctly.

allways _____   allmost _____

allone _____   allready _____

allthough _____   allmighty _____

3. Take the **–al** suffix off each word. Write the root word you are left with.

comical _____   seasonal _____

national _____   musical _____

regional _____   topical _____

tropical _____   logical _____

4. Correctly add **–full** to each of these words.

Use Rule 2 to help you.

use _____   hope _____

power _____   cheer _____

help _____   pain _____

rest _____   thank _____

Test your spelling

Look at the words.

Say them aloud.

Cover the words.

Write them from memory.

Check your spelling.

stall	shell	chill
pull	always	already
powerful	beautiful	
personal	criminal	

The letter strings ci and ti

When the letter strings **ci** and **ti** come within a word, and are followed by **a**, **e** or **o**, they often make a *sh* sound.

musi**ci**an

pre**ci**ous

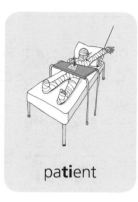

pa**ti**ent

sta**ti**on

Practice activities

1. Complete these words.

```
                        ┌──────────────┬──────┤ ci ├──────┬──────────────┐
                        ↓              ↓              ↓              ↓              ↓
```

spe_____al   musi_____an   an_____ent   suspi_____on   deli_____ous

```
                        ┌──────────────┬──────┤ ti ├──────┬──────────────┐
                        ↓              ↓              ↓              ↓              ↓
```

pa_____ent   ini_____al   essen_____al   infec_____ous   cau_____ous

2. Which of the words in practice activity 1 means:

   a) someone who plays music? _____

   b) absolutely necessary? _____

   c) tasting pleasant? _____

   d) a feeling there is something wrong? _____

   e) able to wait without getting angry? _____

   f) very careful? _____

   g) different from anything else? _____

3. Write a sentence for each of the given words.

Use a dictionary if you are unsure of the meaning of any word.

a) artificial

_____

b) mathematician

_____

c) torrential

_____

d) efficient

_____

e) confidential

_____

f) suspicious

_____

g) cautious

_____

h) physician

_____

Test your spelling

Look at the words.

Say them aloud.

Cover the words.

Write them from memory.

Check your spelling.

social	magician	delicious
suspicion	efficient	patient
initial	cautious	
ambition	subtraction	

Unstressed vowels

Key to spelling

When you say some words, it is hard to hear some of the vowels. These are called **unstressed vowels**.

choc - **o** - late

The second **o** is unstressed in the word **chocolate**.

It is helpful to break words down into syllables and say each syllable to help you remember the spelling of words with unstressed vowels.

Practice activities

1. Complete these words by filling in the missing unstressed vowel in each. The first one has been done for you.

   Use a dictionary if necessary.

   veget<u>a</u>bles   cam__ra

   di__mond   diff__rent

   int__rest   hist__ry

   sep__rate   math__matics

   myst__ry   valu__ble

   comp__ny   temp__rature

Unstressed vowels

2. Each of these words is spelt incorrectly and has an unstressed vowel missing. Rewrite each word correctly.

Use a dictionary if necessary.

dangrous	_____	Wednsday	_____
Janury	_____	marvllous	_____
fastner	_____	delivry	_____
jewellry	_____	freedm	_____
compny	_____	busness	_____
Satrday	_____	Febrary	_____
genrous	_____	gardner	_____
minral	_____	factry	_____
centry	_____	necssary	_____
animl	_____	seprate	_____
intrest	_____	histry	_____
voluntry	_____	offring	_____

Test your spelling

Look at the words.

Say them aloud.

Cover the words.

Write them from memory.

Check your spelling.

interest   jumped   valuable

different   diamond   interesting

vegetable   gardening

history   separate

Vowel endings other than e

Key to spelling

There are many words ending in **e**. There are fewer words ending in the other vowels. Here are some of them:

| camer**a** | kiw**i** | banj**o** | em**u** |

Practice activities

1. Below are some words that have come into our language from Italy. Read them aloud and add them to the table.

pizza	opera
solo	pasta
spaghetti	cello
ravioli	macaroni
piano	risotto

words ending with a	words ending with i	words ending with o

2. Rewrite each of these, adding the correct vowel on the end.

Use a dictionary to help you.

anacond _____	**bong** _____
chapatt _____	**kimon** _____
gn _____	**geck** _____
kiw _____	**banan** _____
radi _____	**armadill** _____
ding _____	**camer** _____
pum _____	**samos** _____
bhaj _____	**em** _____
sof _____	**tarantul** _____

Test your spelling

Look at the words.

Say them aloud.

Cover the words.

Write them from memory.

Check your spelling.

banana	pasta	umbrella
ski	confetti	disco
radio	piano	
emu	gnu	

Prefixes and meanings

Key to spelling

Prefixes have a variety of meanings. These meanings are often defined in good dictionaries.

semi– means half

semicircle = half a circle

Practice activities

1. Choose the correct prefix to go with each of the following, then write the word in full. The first one has been done for you.

    a) sub– or **tele–**

    way _____subway_____   phone _____

    vision _____   marine _____

    b) auto– or **trans–**

    fer _____   biography _____

    late _____   graph _____

    c) circum– or **sur–**

    face _____   plus _____

    stances _____   ference _____

Prefixes and meanings

2. Write the **sub–** word that means:

   a) a boat that goes under the sea   _____

   b) a way or path underground   _____

3. Write the **tele–** word that means:

   a) something that receives pictures from afar   _____

   b) something that receives voices from afar   _____

4. Write the **auto–** or **trans–** word that means:

   a) the story of a person's life written by themselves   _____

   b) to change from one language into another   _____

   c) a person's own signature   _____

   d) to move something from one place to another   _____

5. Write the **circum–** or **sur–** word that means:

   a) the conditions surrounding an event   _____

   b) the outside part of something   _____

   c) the amount left over   _____

   d) the distance around the edge of a circle   _____

Test your spelling

Look at the words.

Say them aloud.

Cover the words.

Write them from memory.

Check your spelling.

submit	subject	television
surpass	transport	transform
telephone	autobiography	
surmount	circumscribe	

Number prefixes

Key to spelling

Some prefixes tell you about numbers.

a **uni**corn

uni– means one

a **bi**cycle

bi– means two

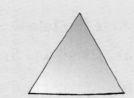

a **tri**angle

tri– means three

Practice activities

1. Write the correct name of each cycle.

_____　　　_____　　　_____

2. Write a definition for each of these words.

   Use a dictionary to help you.

   a) unicorn

   _____

   b) unison

   _____

   c) unify

   _____

   d) unique

   _____

3. Match each **bi–** word with its correct meaning.

Use a dictionary if necessary.

bicycle   **bilingual**   **bisect**   **biped**

a) to cut into two parts   _____

b) speaks two languages   _____

c) an animal with two feet   _____

d) a vehicle with two wheels   _____

4. Match each **tri–** word with its correct meaning.

Use a dictionary if necessary.

triangle   **tricycle**   **trio**   **triple**

a) to multiply by three   _____

b) a shape with three sides   _____

c) a group of three   _____

d) a vehicle with three wheels   _____

Test your spelling

Look at the words.

Say them aloud.

Cover the words.

Write them from memory.

Check your spelling.

unit	unify	uniform
universe	bisect	bicycle
biannual	triangle	
tripod	trident	

Anglo-Saxon prefixes

Key to spelling

Many words in the English language originate from a long time ago and from other languages. Lots of prefixes originate from the Anglo-Saxon period of our history.

misfortune

The Anglo-Saxon prefix **mis–** means **wrong** or **bad**. Fortune means good luck, so misfortune means bad luck.

befriend

One meaning of the Anglo-Saxon prefix **be–** is **to make**. To befriend someone means to make friends with them.

Practice activities

1. Add **mis–** or **be–** to make some new words.

    a) grudge   _____

    b) witch   _____

    c) manage   _____

    d) spell   _____

    e) use   _____

    f) calm   _____

Anglo-Saxon prefixes

2. Use the answers you gave in practice activity 1 to help you write the **mis–** or **be–** word that means:

   a) to make calm _____

   b) to manage badly _____

   c) to use something wrongly _____

   d) to spell incorrectly _____

3. Complete this table by finding a word for each prefix.

   Use a dictionary to help you.

Anglo-Saxon prefix	meaning	example word
a–	on	
fore–	before	
off–	from	
out–	beyond	
over–	over, beyond	
un–	not	
with–	back, against	

Test your spelling

Look at the words.

Say them aloud.

Cover the words.

Write them from memory.

Check your spelling.

aboard   befriend   forecast

misplace   offspring   overthrow

withhold   withstand

outlaw   unaided

More Anglo-Saxon words

Key to spelling

It was not only prefixes that the Anglo-Saxons gave to our language. Many words, or parts of words, used today originate from Anglo-Saxon times more than 1000 years ago.

The word **bandage** comes from the Anglo-Saxon word **bindan**, which means to bind.

Practice activities

1. Some Anglo-Saxon words look very similar to our modern words. Here are some words in sets. Write what you think the modern word is for each Anglo-Saxon word. The first one has been done for you.

   Family words

   moder   _____mother_____   faeder   _____

   sweoster   _____   brothor   _____

   sunu   _____   dohter   _____

   Colour words

   blew   _____   read   _____

   hwit   _____   brun   _____

   silfer   _____   geolo   _____

2. Match the Anglo-Saxon words to their modern English equivalents. The first one has been done for you.

a) hors   dog

b) gat   sheep

c) docga   cat

d) wulf   horse

e) sceap   wolf

3. Match these Anglo-Saxon words with the related words from modern English. The first one has been done for you.

a) floetan (to float)   learn, lore

b) sceran (to cut)   fleet, afloat

c) faran (to go)   wisdom, witness

d) beran (to carry)   scrape, share

e) wegan (to move)   far, ferry

f) laeran (to teach)   barrow, burden

g) witan (to know)   wagon, weigh

Test your spelling

Look at the words.

Say them aloud.

Cover the words.

Write them from memory.

Check your spelling.

quicken	steady	fodder
twin	two	weigh
food	share	
wise	quicksand	

Anglo-Saxon suffixes

Key to spelling

Many suffixes also originate from the Anglo-Saxon period of our history.

darken

drummer

The suffix **–en** can mean **to make**. Dark**en** therefore means to make dark.

Sometimes the spelling of the root word remains the same when the suffix is added.

The suffix **–er** often means a do**er** of something. A farm**er** is therefore someone who farms.

Sometimes the spelling of the root word is changed slightly when the suffix is added.

Practice activities

1. Make some words by adding suffixes.

    Add **–en** to these words.

    quick _____   **soft** _____

    bright _____   **light** _____

    Add **–er** to these words.

    box _____   **print** _____

    teach _____   **garden** _____

2. Take the suffix off these words. Work out the root words.

    fatten _____   **shaven** _____

    whiten _____   **worrier** _____

3. Here are some more words with common Anglo-Saxon suffixes. Match up the pairs of words according to their suffixes. Underline the common suffix in each word. The first one has been done for you.

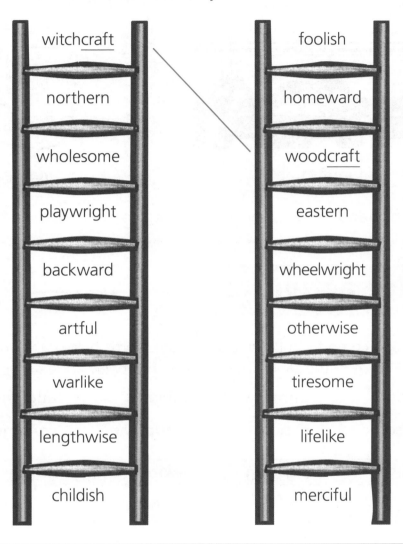

witch<u>craft</u>	foolish
northern	homeward
wholesome	wood<u>craft</u>
playwright	eastern
backward	wheelwright
artful	otherwise
warlike	tiresome
lengthwise	lifelike
childish	merciful

Test your spelling

Look at the words.

Say them aloud.

Cover the words.

Write them from memory.

Check your spelling.

freedom	fellowship	woollen
twofold	earthen	manifold
uppermost	lordship	
kingdom	topmost	

Latin words

Many words, or parts of words, in our language come from Latin.

manufacture

manuscript

manus means **hand** in Latin. The words above come from it.

Practice activities

1. Many prefixes come from Latin. Look at the words below and write them in the correct place in the table. The first one has been done for you.

aquarium	primary	subway	audience
supersonic	expel	aeroplane	conjunction

Latin prefix	meaning	word that includes the prefix
prim–	first	primary
aero–	air	
aqua–	water	
audi–	hearing	
sub–	under	
ex–	out	
con–	together	
super–	above	

2. Match these Latin words with the related words from modern English. The first one has been done for you.

a) amo (I love) —————————————— dental

b) corpus (body) ———————————— amiable

c) dentis (tooth)   current

d) moveo (I move)   manufacture

e) pendeo (I hang)   reside

f) tempus (time)   captain

g) sedeo (I sit)   corpse

h) caput (head)   penalty

i) curro (I run)   proverb

j) manus (hand)   temporary

k) poena (punishment)   pendulum

l) verbum (word)   movement

Test your spelling

Look at the words.

Say them aloud.

Cover the words.

Write them from memory.

Check your spelling.

describe	signal	spectator
evident	scribble	reflection
vision	signature	
flexible	inspection	

Latin suffixes

Many suffixes originate from Latin. Understanding the meaning of a particular suffix may help you to understand the meaning and spelling of the whole word.

comfort**able**

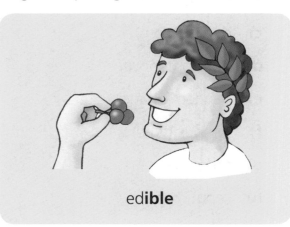

ed**ible**

The suffixes **–able** and **–ible** both mean **capable of**.

Comfort**able** means capable of giving comfort.

Ed**ible** means capable of being eaten.

Practice activities

1. Rewrite these correctly with an **–able** or **–ible** suffix.

   Use a dictionary to help you.

   fashion _____   **invis** _____

   respons _____   **suit** _____

   reason _____   **remark** _____

   horr _____   **flex** _____

2. Remove the suffix from each of these words and spell the root word correctly.

   Use a dictionary to help you.

   valuable _____   **reliable** _____

   deplorable _____   **movable** _____

   memorable _____   **usable** _____

3. Here are some more words with common Latin suffixes. Write the root word and write a sentence containing the suffixed word.

a) leakage   _____

_____

b) assistant   _____

_____

c) gigantic   _____

_____

d) mountaineer   _____

_____

e) familiar   _____

_____

f) signify   _____

_____

g) justice   _____

_____

h) reliable   _____

_____

Test your spelling

Look at the words.

Say them aloud.

Cover the words.

Write them from memory.

Check your spelling.

famous	capture	attitude
intricate	delicate	composure
necessary	venomous	
fortitude	momentary	

Greek words

Practice activities

1. Many prefixes come from Greek. Think of a word for each prefix and complete the table. The first one has been done for you.

   Use a dictionary to help you.

Greek prefix	meaning	word that includes the prefix
anti–	against	antiseptic
arch–	chief	
auto–	self	
para–	beside	
tele–	from afar	
micro–	small	
photo–	light	
dia–	through	

Greek words

2. Match these Greek words with the related words from modern English. The first one has been done for you.

a) aster (star) —————————— cosmetic

b) grapho (I write) ——————— astrology

c) logos (word/speech)   dialogue

d) pathos (suffering)   telescope

e) polis (city)   pathetic

f) gramma (thing written)   biology

g) sphaira (globe)   autograph

h) bios (life)   melody

i) kosmos (beauty)   sphere

j) metron (a measure)   optician

k) phone (sound)   politics

l) skopeo (I see)   grammar

m) oide (a song)   metre

n) optikus (to do with sight)   microphone

Test your spelling

Look at the words.

Say them aloud.

Cover the words.

Write them from memory.

Check your spelling.

autograph	phonics	economy
anagram	symphony	geology
telegram	microscope	
geography	astronomy	

French words

Key to spelling

A lot of words used in English have been borrowed from the French language. Many words taken from French contain the letters **ch**.

A **chef** works in a restaurant.

The word ending **–et** also often indicates that a word comes from French.

Practice activities

1. Rewrite the incomplete words below with an **–et** ending.

   duv _____   trump _____

   crick _____   cabar _____

   ball _____   scarl _____

   brack _____   bouqu _____

   tick _____   buff _____

2. Say the words you have made in practice activity 1 aloud. Add them to the table below. Two have been done for you.

–et sounds like *ay* as in day	–et sounds like *et* as in wet
duvet	trumpet

3. Write the **–et** word from practice activity 1 that means:

   a) a type of dance _____

   b) a variety of entertainments _____

   c) a bed covering _____

4. Read aloud the words below and listen to the sound the **ch** makes. Write a sentence for each given word.

   a) parachute

   _____

   b) chef

   _____

   c) brochure

   _____

   d) sachet

   _____

   e) machine

   _____

Test your spelling

Look at the words.

Say them aloud.

Cover the words.

Write them from memory.

Check your spelling.

bracket	trumpet	duvet
ballet	sachet	chef
machine	brochure	
souvenir	promenade	

The history of words

Key to spelling

As you will have seen from page 62 onwards, some of our words have fascinating histories! Understanding a little about the origins of words may help you to remember them better.

Wednesday

This day is named after Woden, a Viking god.

March

This month is named after Mars, the Roman god of war.

Practice activities

1. Which day do you think was named after:

   a) Tiw, a Viking god?   _____

   b) Frig, a Viking goddess?   _____

   c) Thor, a god of thunder?   _____

   d) the Sun?   _____

   e) Saturn, a Roman god?   _____

   f) the Moon?   _____

2. Which month do you think was named after:

   a) the Roman Emperor Augustus?   _____

   b) Maia, the Roman goddess of spring?   _____

   c) Janus, a two-faced god?   _____

   d) the Roman Emperor Julius Caesar?   _____

   e) the chief Roman goddess, Juno?   _____

3. Write which month you think comes from each of these Roman numbers.

    a) septem (seven)   _____

    b) octo (eight)   _____

    c) novem (nine)   _____

    d) decem (ten)   _____

4. Eponyms are words that have originated from people's names. For example, the guillotine is named after Dr Joseph Guillotin. Write the meaning of each of these words. Can you find out how each word originated?

    a) biro

    _____

    _____

    b) diesel

    _____

    _____

    c) pasteurise

    _____

    _____

Test your spelling

Look at the words.

Say them aloud.

Cover the words.

Write them from memory.

Check your spelling.

Wednesday	**Saturday**	**February**
August	**December**	**pasteurise**
diesel	**January**	
Tuesday	**Thursday**	

Confusing words

Key to spelling

Many confusing words are **homophones** or near-homophones – they are spelt differently, but sound very similar.

device
a noun

devise
a verb

In such pairs of words, nouns often end with **ce** and verbs with **se**.

It is useful to remember that in pairs of words such as **device** and **devise**, the verb is pronounced with a **z** sound. This cannot be spelt with a **c**.

Practice activities

1. Look at these nouns. Write the verb (with the **se** ending) and then write a sentence containing either the verb or the noun.

    a) advice _____

    _____

    b) device _____

    _____

    c) licence _____

    _____

    d) practice _____

    _____

78

2. Use a dictionary to help you to write a definition for each of the homophones.

a) heard

_____

b) herd

_____

c) ascent

_____

d) assent

_____

e) profit

_____

f) prophet

_____

g) aisle

_____

h) isle

_____

i) farther

_____

j) father

_____

Test your spelling

Look at the words.

Say them aloud.

Cover the words.

Write them from memory.

Check your spelling.

advise	advice	aisle
isle	heard	herd
ascent	assent	
farther	father	

More confusing words

Key to spelling

It is important to not only know how to spell near-homophones, but also to be able to distinguish between their different meanings.

eliminate

to get rid of

illuminate

to light up

Practice activities

1. Look at each pair of near-homophones. Write each near-homophone and a definition.

   Use a dictionary to help you.

   a) affect; effect

   _____

   _____

   b) desert; dessert

   _____

   _____

   c) eligible; illegible

   _____

   _____

   d) guest; guessed

   _____

   _____

More confusing words

2. Find the pairs of homophones in the words below and rewrite them together. The first one has been done for you.

who's	aloud	steal	altar
led	bridal	stationary	bridle
allowed	cereal	compliment	descent
lead	serial	complement	steel
stationery	whose	dissent	alter

who's   whose   _____   _____

_____   _____   _____   _____

_____   _____   _____   _____

_____   _____   _____   _____

_____   _____   _____   _____

3. Write a sentence containing the words **guest** and **guessed**.

Use a dictionary to help you to use the words correctly.

_____

_____

Test your spelling

Look at the words.

Say them aloud.

Cover the words.

Write them from memory.

Check your spelling.

desert	dessert	cereal
serial	descent	dissent
compliment	complement	
who's	whose	

More words to practise

This is an additional list of words, not covered in the *Test your spelling* sections, which you should also practise and learn to spell in Years 5 and 6. Like you did in the *Test your spelling* sections, practise them by **looking** at the words, **saying** them aloud, **covering** the words, **writing** them from memory and **checking** your spelling.

accommodate	accompany	according	aggressive
amateur	ancient	apparent	appreciate
atmosphere	attached	available	average
awkward	bargain	believe	boundary
bruise	career	category	celebrate
cemetery	century	challenge	committee
communicate	community	competition	conscience
controversy	convenience	convince	correspond
criticise	curiosity	deprive	desperate
destroy	determined	develop	dictionary
disastrous	embarrass	emigrate	encourage
endure	engineer	enrol	envelope
environment	equator	equip (–ped, –ment)	especially
estimate	Europe	exaggerate	excavate
exceed	excellent	existence	explanation
forbid	foreign	forty	frequently
fruit	germ	government	gradual
granite	guarantee	harass	haughty
haunt	hearty	height	hinder
hindrance	horizon	humility	hurricane
identity	imagine	immediately	immense

More words to practise

impress	imprison	include	index
individual	influence	inhabitant	instrument
interfere	interrupt	interview	introduce
language	legend	leisure	length
lenient	lightning	liquid	marvellous
medium	military	mineral	mischief
mischievous	modest	moisture	mosquito
muscle	neighbour	nuisance	occupy
occur	omit	opinion	opportunity
parliament	permanent	persevere	persuade
phrase	physical	popular	prejudice
privilege	profession	programme	pronunciation
protect	punctual	purpose	query
queue	rapid	realise	receipt
recent	recognise	recommend	remove
request	resemble	resign	restaurant
restore	revise	rhyme	rhythm
ridiculous	sacrifice	saucepan	scheme
secretary	shoulder	sign	sincere(ly)
society	soldier	sphere	statue
stomach	stubborn	style	succeed
sufficient	suggest	suit	superior
surprise	syllable	symbol	sympathy
syrup	system	talent	telescope
temperature	tempt	terminate	theatre

More words to practise

triumph	twelfth	twelve	tyrant
utter	vacant	variety	vehicle
ventilate	villain	volcano	volume
wardrobe	whether	wisdom	wizard
wrench	yeast	yacht	zoology

Test practice

The tests here will help you to see how well you know your spelling. They provide practice for the spelling task at the end of Key Stage 2. (N.B. The spelling task in the KS2 SATs will have 20 words to find).
- Each sentence has a word missing.
- Ask somebody to read each missing word and sentence to you (these can be found in the answer booklet).
- Write the missing word in the space provided, making sure you spell it correctly.

Test 1

1. She can _____ very fast.

2. They _____ that the sea was cold.

3. I think I can see _____ under the tree.

4. The lost keys were at the police _____.

5. He found the maths test _____.

6. I _____ pocket money cleaning the car.

7. She is so _____.

8. Dogs are not _____ in the shop.

9. In my _____ they are silly.

10. I will _____ you to join our club.

Test 2

1. Please help me to _____ the wood.

2. It is really _____ to see you again.

3. I will do it _____ I return.

4. They took so much _____ from the letter.

5. Be quiet so you do not _____ the baby.

6. Her ideas are good, but her _____ lets her down.

7. I must return the book to the _____.

8. It pays to be _____ when walking on ice.

9. The pest control officer was called to _____ the rats.

10. A lovely _____ sailed past the beach.

Test practice

Test 3

1. _____ food is excellent.

2. I need to know which _____ to call.

3. Please leave the bag in my _____.

4. Let's start at the very _____.

5. It was a _____ wet day.

6. I woke up too _____ today.

7. We need _____ help.

8. The whole story was _____.

9. There was a _____ gift awaiting them.

10. They could only _____ how long it would take.

Test 4

1. Do not walk through the _____.

2. We _____ to lie on the beach.

3. _____ is a great film showing tonight.

4. I have a _____ idea than you.

5. The day ended _____ for all involved.

6. The robber had a cunning _____.

7. Showing them the tickets is sure to _____ them.

8. Keep away from others as you are still _____.

9. Please do not _____ our progress.

10. Let's go to the _____ tonight.

The next two tests are longer – they each have 20 words to find – in order to match the length of the spelling task in the Key Stage 2 SATs.

Test 5

1. Make sure you do not _____ on the cracks.

2. It will be _____ own fault if they miss the bus.

3. We can only _____ we get there on time.

4. _____ the width of the window carefully.

5. There was a _____ shortage of petrol.

6. It is _____ to think you can jump over that.

7. I will be back _____ I need to collect my things.

8. He did not want to be _____ by the others.

9. The parachute jump was a great _____.

10. We must _____ our shooting and passing.

11. If you cannot hear, just _____ the volume.

12. I _____ we would be there by now.

13. It is a _____ sum of money to share.

14. They _____ to go swimming.

15. The necklace had a very _____ diamond pendant.

16. Everyone was being very _____ in the line.

17. Cycling is very _____ in the summer months.

18. We can _____ with each other by email.

19. _____ is used to make bread rise.

20. There was a very _____ incident at lunchtime.

Test practice

Test 6

1. Let's _____ some cakes.

2. They all went to look at the _____.

3. Open the _____ to let the cat out.

4. The pop group were _____ superstars.

5. The new boy in Year 1 has a _____ in Year 3.

6. They always show great _____ in the chocolate cakes.

7. The first thing we will do is _____ the area.

8. It was an incredible flying _____.

9. When I grow up, I might be _____.

10. She was very _____ about going to her new school.

11. A _____ looking dog snarled from behind the fence.

12. Let everyone _____ so they can get to assembly.

13. _____ it was raining, they still had great fun.

14. The book was in _____ condition.

15. The decorator stood on a ladder to paint the _____.

16. The chef created a _____ meal.

17. It was her _____ to walk to school.

18. It is a great _____ to meet the Queen.

19. I could hear the _____ buzzing around the room.

20. Britain is an island in northern _____.

The practice activities in this book will have helped you to learn many words. There will, of course, be some spellings which you will still find difficult, so it is important to keep practising. Revisit the *Test your spelling* sections that appear throughout the book to help build your confidence.